Whether you're going to find out through this guide that perhaps your dog is one for whom the Dog Park is not appropriate, whether you're going to find out through this guide when to remove your appropriate dog from the Dog Park for his own protection, or whether you're going to find a great play group for your dog, I hope the words contained in this manual can help you keep your dog (and other dogs) safe, happy, and healthy.

Out and About With Your Dog

Book design: Brian Peterson

Printed in the United States

OUT AND ABOUT WITH YOUR DOG

Dog to Dog Interactions

on the street, on the trails
and in the dog park

Sue Sternberg

CONTENTS

SECTION ONE:

On the street, on the trails

SECTION TWO:

In the Dog Park

SECTION ONE

Introduction

Many dogs are angels in their own homes, angels with humans, but behavioral nightmares when in the presence of other dogs. And even if your dog means no harm, the sight and sound of a dog lunging and growling at the end of his leash trying to get to another dog causes the public to panic, make wide berths or cross the streets to avoid your dog—the dog they believe to be horribly evil and aggressive. Some dogs can actually play well off leash with other dogs, but on leash, become snarling, lunging monsters. Owners of these alleged monsters are shunned, ostracized, looked down upon, and believed to be at fault and the reason for their dog's bad behaviors.

Does your dog lunge and strain and bark when you're out on a walk and another dog appears? Does it feel embarrassing to be out in public with your dog if any other dogs are around? Has your dog picked fights at the public Dog Park? Is your dog a heat-seeking missile that really does hate all other dogs?

Or does your dog seem to love other dogs so much that any other dog in his sight causes him to pull and strain and gag and claw his way towards it?

It can be just as frustrating to live with a dog who LOVES playing with other dogs, because he loves them so much that he feels the need to strain and pull towards any other dog he sees while out on a walk. Sometimes, a dog who adores other dogs so much that he is out of control around them is as difficult or embarrassing to live with as a dog who hates other dogs.

No matter what particular behavior your dog displays around other dogs, this book will offer training and management tips so that your dog can behave like a good canine citizen in the presence of other dogs.

CHAPTER ONE
On-Leash Encounters

ON–LEASH ENCOUNTERS

The absolute hardest, most problematic, most difficult way for dogs to greet and meet is on leash. And there are really only two potential outcomes for the greeting, and neither is particularly useful or desirable:

1. After the initial investigative sniffing and greeting ritual, the dogs play.

2. After the initial investigative sniffing and greeting ritual, the dogs fight.

Neither is actually better than the other. If the dogs sniff and then play, your dog has just gotten a jackpot sized reward for going up to a strange dog and introducing himself. The next time he sees a strange dog, he will want to pull towards that dog to greet it, to see if he can make a friend and have a little play session. Each subsequent time, your dog will strain harder and harder to get to the other dogs, hoping to get to stop and play. If nothing else, this will lead to a harder and harder time managing your dog on walks, since he now gets so distracted around other dogs. Also, if your dog mostly plays when he greets other dogs, but suddenly meets a dog that tries to fight him, your dog can quickly learn not to trust oncoming dogs, and not to trust himself in meeting and greeting other dogs. Sometimes this leads to a dog that preemptively lashes out at other, on-coming dogs, and a perfectly friendly dog transforms into a snarling, lunging monster. You'll also stop trusting owners who tell you that their dog is 'friendly' when half the time their dog clearly is not.

If the dogs sniff and then squabble, or actually fight, then your dog could either start to fear other dogs when he sees them on the street, or worse, he will begin to pull towards them, wanting to pick a fight.

You basically get the same problematic dog either outcome. Whether fighting or playing, on-leash encounters usually produce a dog that pulls and strains and often lunges to get to other dogs. The motivation may be different (I want to play, I want to fight) but the symptom is the same: your dog becomes more and more of a nightmare to walk in public.

TEACH YOUR DOG TO IGNORE OTHER DOGS

It's best to avoid the possibilities all together, by teaching your dog to ignore other dogs completely when walking on leash, unless specifically stopped on command, told to 'sit' and 'stay' and wait for permission to approach and greet. Otherwise, your dog should learn that when he's on leash, he should walk past and ignore other dogs.

The best plan of action for on leash encounters is plain and simple: if your dog is on a leash, you should avoid contact with other dogs, leashed or unleashed. There is no need for your leashed dog to learn how to greet other dogs politely, successfully, or at all. As long as your dog can ignore other dogs, he does not need to be able to GO UP to another dog and greet and meet another dog politely or in a playful manner in order to be a good canine citizen.

13

GETTING PAST ANOTHER DOG ON THE SIDEWALK

Many dogs can stride out at the end of their leashes, sniff about, and walk casually and calmly as other dogs pass by. Many dogs cannot.

These different types of dogs are mostly born, not made, which you'll believe if and when you get the type that cannot walk past another dog without lunging and barking. If you have the easy dog, one that can be ignored in the presence of other dogs and still behave, lucky you. Just wait.

For the rest of us with dogs that go deaf and escalate into horrifying beasts in the presence of other dogs, here are some training steps. Dogs who behave in beastly ways do not need more 'socialization' with other dogs. They need to be taught—actively taught—how to ignore other dogs. They don't and won't do it naturally. They won't just 'get used' to other dogs. In fact, practicing the lunging and barking over and over again will make the dog worse. Practice does make perfect. Be proactive and help your dog practice acceptable behavior, not aggressive displays.

? *So how can you help your dog walk nonchalantly past another dog he encounters on the sidewalk?*

YOUR DOG WILL NEED THREE NEW SKILLS:

1. The ability to look up at your face at your command, and continue staring at you (and nothing but you) until you give him permission to look away.

2. The ability to heel at your left side, matching your stride, his head tilted upwards and his eyes staring up at your face as you pass another dog.

3. The ability to heel at your right side, matching your stride, his head tilted upwards and his eyes staring up at your face as you pass another dog.

If the oncoming dog will end up passing you on your left side, then your dog will need to heel on your right side, so that you create a blockade between them. Conversely, if the oncoming dog will end up passing on your right side, your dog will need to heel on your left side.

TEACHING YOUR DOG TO PAY ATTENTION AND STARE AT YOU WHEN YOU REQUEST IT

It goes without saying that if your dog is looking at you, paying attention to you, he cannot simultaneously be looking at another dog. In order to stop your dog from misbehaving, first you'll have to teach a desirable alternative behavior. It can't just be the absence of a bad behavior—dogs don't understand voids. Dogs need active behaviors they can perform in place of bad behaviors. If your dog could act naturally and calmly around other dogs he would. He can't. He needs something else to do and it must be taught, step by step. And it must be taught in the quiet of your own home and yard, without any distractions. The new, alternative behavior must be ingrained into your dog's head for at least two weeks before expecting him to be able to listen to you in the presence of another dog. Once a dog's state of mind has surpassed a certain level of arousal, he becomes oblivious to your commands, oblivious to everything except the other dog. At his peak of arousal and misbehavior, your dog is deaf, will not eat treats, and does feel any tugging on the leash. And he becomes possessed.

He certainly cannot learn a new behavior at his peak of arousal. He needs his classroom to be inside his home where he's calm and comfortable. His learning environment needs to be your yard absent of any distractions.

TIPS:

If he sniffs your treats before eating, or refuses to eat altogether, he's either not hungry enough or your treats aren't tempting enough. Skip one of his meals or get more creative with your treats.

Reward any freely offered attention from your dog throughout the day, indoors or out. Smile, mark this great attention with a hearty and appreciative "yes" and then praise and pet your dog. He needs to know that the more he looks at you, the better his life (and your life) will be.

If he looks away for any reason, you're not feeding him often enough—speed it up!

TRAINING PLAN:

BEFORE YOU BEGIN:

Have many different types of treats with you at any training session. The best treats are just that: real treats, not boring bits of biscuits. Try cutting up string cheese, hotdogs, use tortellini. Use small pieces. Cut back on your dog's normal meal portions to compensate for the extra calories training will incur. The more treats you use and the more frequently you give them during the initial foundation training, the stronger your behavior will be in the end. Don't skimp. Start by training inside your own home. Then outside your own home in familiar territory, with no other dogs as distractions. Then, outside in unfamiliar territory with no other dogs as distractions. Then, outside in unfamiliar territory with other dogs waaaaaaaaay waaaaaaaaaay in the distance as distractions. Gradually move your training sessions closer and closer in proximity to other dogs.

THE STEPS:

1. Keep your dog on leash (even if you're training indoors) and wait until he is distracted and sniffing something or looking away.

2. With both hands, find your dog's nose and lure him to you until you have your dog sitting in front of you dead-on, his toes almost touching your toes.

3. Have many tiny treats ready in one hand, and shovel them into your dog, one at a time, until he is looking at you, sitting, and there is a constant stream of treats going into his mouth.

4. Before you run out of treats completely, put away your food, walk away from your dog and ignore him for a few moments. Leave him wanting more, while there's still more to be had.

5. Train for an engrossing 30–45 seconds, then ignore him, wait a few minutes, go to him, and repeat the above sequence.

6. Bring him into a different room and repeat. And then another room and repeat.

7. Bring him outside in a quiet place and repeat.

8. Bring him to your local park or public area, away from other dogs, and repeat.

9. Each time, train intensively and then, before running out of treats, put your dog away.

TEACHING LEFT–SIDE HEELING

This is a moving exercise, meaning your dog is learning to move with you, and therefore it must be taught while moving. Because this is hard to execute, it is easiest to introduce by moving in slow motion.

• Keep your dog on leash (even if you're training indoors). Wait until he is distracted and sniffing something or looking away.

• Take a handful of treats into your right hand and place one big piece in your left hand. Your right hand serves merely as a container.

• Using your left hand as a lure, lure your dog's nose and maneuver him into heel position. This means he is aligned at your side, both your toes and his are facing the same direction, his right shoulder is touching your left leg.

• As soon as he is in the correct position, take a slow motion step forward with your left foot first, and feed your dog the treat that is in your lure hand.

• When your left hand delivers the treat, your dog should be in the position you desire: Place your food on your left leg at the height that, when your dog comes close enough to eat it, puts him in correct "heel" position.

• Make sure you stand up straight and shovel treat after treat into his mouth, so many so rapidly in a row that he is glued to your side and never disengages.

• Keep moving! Reward your dog as you shuffle along at an extremely slow pace, but remember that your dog needs to be fed while moving, since we're teaching him to move with you.

• Before you run out of food, end the exercise by saying "okay" and walking away from your dog. Ignore him for a few minutes.

You'll need at least 2 weeks to really practice this with your dog in many new settings, and without huge distractions—like other dogs.

TEACHING RIGHT–SIDE HEELING

This is a moving exercise, meaning your dog is learning to move with you, and therefore it must be taught while moving. Because this is hard to execute, it is easiest to introduce it while moving in slow motion.

• Keep your dog on leash (even if you're training indoors). Wait until he is distracted and sniffing something or looking away.

• Take a handful of treats into your left hand and place one big piece in your right hand. Your left hand serves merely as a container.

• Using your right hand as a lure, lure your dog's nose and maneuver him into heel position. This means he is aligned at your side, both your toes and his are facing the same direction, his left shoulder is touching your right leg.

• As soon as he is in the correct position, take a slow motion step forward with your right foot first, and feed your dog the treat that is in your lure hand.

• Immediately (so quickly that he doesn't even drop his head to swallow) with your right hand, reach across your body into your container hand and feed your dog another treat, and then another, and then another.

• When your right hand delivers the treat, your dog should be in the position you desire: Put your food on your right leg at the

TIPS

Remember to feed your dog while you are both in motion. If you inadvertently pause to feed him, you are actually teaching him stand in heel position instead. Be generous. Make sure you're not taking your treat and going to your dog's mouth, but rather you're having your dog move into the perfect position alongside your leg to meet your hand and receive his treat.

You'll need at least 2 weeks to really practice this with your dog in many new settings, and without huge distractions—like other dogs.

20

height that, when your dog comes close enough to eat it, puts him in correct "heel" position.

• Make sure you stand up straight and shovel treat after treat into his mouth, so many so rapidly in a row that he is glued to your side and never disengages.

• Keep moving! Reward your dog as you shuffle along at an extremely slow pace, but remember that your dog needs to be fed while moving, since we're teaching him to move with you.

• Before you run out of food, end the exercise by saying "okay" and walking away from your dog. Ignore him for a few minutes.

GETTING RID OF THE TREAT AS A LURE

Heeling your dog successfully past another dog while out in public is certainly your goal, but for many die-hard lungers, you may be chained to luring shamelessly each time to keep their attention on you.

Others, with dogs less committed to eradicating all dogs from the planet, can eventually achieve a more permanent, more independent heel-past-another-dog.

Even if you one day accidentally find yourself out in public with an approaching dog, and you have no treats on you (it's guaranteed to happen—it's called real life), assume the exact position with your hands and draw your dog over to you and move briskly past. You can fool many a dog that has had a solid foundation of training.

If there's no fooling your dog, if you're caught unprepared, immediately execute a sharp about-turn (turning away from your dog) and walk as fast as you can in the opposite

direction you were going. This will put you in front of
the approaching dog, who will now be following you,
but this gives you time to scout ahead for a barrier to
hide behind as you let the dog pass.

WEANING OFF THE FOOD LURE
(not the food reward):

•After luring with food in your hand for at least three of
these sessions, keep all the treats in your left hand, and
lure (with your fingers in exactly the same position as if
they were holding an actual treat but they're not, they're
empty) your dog into heel position, move forward one
step, and IMMEDIATELY reach into your left hand for a
jackpot of treats.

•Once you have done this successfully with no treat in
your lure-hand, DO NOT LURE AGAIN WITH FOOD
IN YOUR HAND. BUT—always
reward from the lure hand after
the behavior.

•Do not start randomizing your
treats yet. Your dog must first learn
to faithfully follow your hand even
though he sees no food. Which
means he must be rewarded, after
the fact, WITH FOOD (in fact
MORE food than he would have
gotten following one measly treat)
when he does the desired behavior.

•Repeat this same exercise by
switching hands and sides, so that
your dog is equally comfortable
working in either right or left side
heel position.

TIPS:

*When you reach down to feed
your dog, flip your wrist, so
that you end up with "gorilla"
knuckles: knuckles facing for-
wards, wrists bent, palms facing in the direction behind you.
From this "gorilla" position you
can keep your lure arm tight
against your body and lure
your dog into a nice, neat and
close heel position.*

THE PUBLIC BAIL–OUT MANEUVER:

Sometimes, trying to heel past another dog is too challenging. Sometimes the space is so narrow that you'd be so close to the other dog that your own dog won't be able to listen to you. Sometimes the approaching dog is unsafe, out of control, or most annoying, off leash and out of control.

When this happens (and it will) you'll need to back perpendicularly away from the line of travel, and back away as far as you can go, or back up until you're behind a barrier. You'll stand facing the approaching dog, your dog will be sitting in front of you with his back to the oncoming dog, and you will be shoveling food treats one after the other into your dog's mouth.

THE STEPS:

1. Keep your dog on leash (even if you're training indoors) wait until he is distracted and sniffing something or looking away.

2. Using two hands, with food in both, back yourself up a few paces, lure your dog's nose in front of you, so that he is facing you, his nose touching your pants, and stop.

3. You may have to draw the lure upwards a few inches as your dog gets close.

4. Ask your dog to "sit".

5. With a treat in both hands, feed your dog rapidly one treat after another.

6. Before you run out of treats, tell your dog "okay" and walk away and ignore your dog.

You'll need at least 2 weeks to really practice this with your dog in many new settings, and without huge distractions—like other dogs.

23

CHAPTER TWO
Enjoying the Great Outdoors With Your Dog

Our relationship with dogs allows us access into life in the present. The here and now. You give your dog some of his greatest gifts when you take him with you in a partnered activity in the outdoors.

All too often life for a dog is frustrating and under-stimulating. Restricted on a six-foot leash with an owner who neither walks nor runs as fast as he does. If an owner has a fenced yard, a dog will explore its boundaries, like being stuck in a fish tank, and he's usually alone when in his yard. Rarely is his exercise or much of his life a team activity with his owner.

If we as dog owners want to keep our access to trails alive, each one of us must assume the role of ambassadors for dog owners everywhere.

GETTING PAST ANOTHER DOG ON THE TRAILS

If you enjoy walking or hiking outdoors on the trails with your dog, you'll need some maneuvers to help keep or train your dog to be a welcome canine trail-user. Outdoor hiking/walking (or even biking) with your dog can present some different problems than just walking in a neighborhood on a sidewalk.

On the trails, you are more likely to encounter other dogs off–leash than you are in urban or suburban neighborhoods. And with those off–leash dogs come the inevitable "But he's friendly..." calls from owners of those off–leash dogs. Nothing is more irritating to the responsible owner with his dog on–leash than the off–leash (and so–often out of control and NOT so friendly) dog. Rarely, it seems, does the owner of that off–leash dog even carry a leash, and even more rarely does the owner of the off–leash dog have any semblance of a reliable "Come Here" command. Which leaves you, the owner of the leashed dog, who may or may not be well–behaved around other dogs, at the mercy of the encounter.

You'll want to train in the "Bail Out" technique (explained on page 12) as well as the 'Left Side' and 'Right Side' (explained on pages 8 and 9 respectively).

TRAIL MANNERS:

Access to the great outdoors with our dogs is a gift, and should be treated with appreciation and great respect. There are less and less opportunities for dog owners to share the great outdoors with our dogs.

Training and practicing with your dog while out on the trails isn't just about improving your dog's behavior—it also serves to announce good doggie trail manners. It impresses, relieves and relaxes other trail users. Not everyone loves dogs. Many people are afraid, some phobic, of dogs.

The more positive experiences other trail users have with us dog owners, the more welcome we will remain on trails.

CANINE TRAIL ETIQUETTE:

1. Whenever someone passes, step off the trail, gather your dog to you, and place your dog at your side farthest away from the other trail users while you wait for them to pass.

2. Clean up all poop—turds that land on the trail or on the side of the trail need to be bagged up and carried out, or bring your own bag and carry it out, or take two sticks and 'chopstick' the poop well off the trails!

3. Clean up other dogs' messes, too, as everyone will still think it's your dog's mess anyway, even if it isn't.

4. Move over and stop whenever someone passes, or at the very least move your dog off the trail and place yourself between your dog and the other trail users.

5. Always carry a leash! And use it whenever you are in the vicinity of anyone else.

6. If you don't have voice control of your dog, keep him on a leash until he has more training.

7. If your dog has any barking issues or aggression problems with strangers, children, or other dogs, your dog does not belong off-leash, EVER.

8. If your dog is not 100% reliable when you call him to you, keep him on leash and consider further training.

A HIERARCHY OF TRAIL USERS:

People come first—in consideration of our fellow trail users, our dogs should be the lowest ranking members of these trails.

On busy trails, when many other trail users are passing from all directions, your dog should be kept on your right side, or moved to your right side each and every time someone passes. If there are frequent trail users coming up from behind to pass, dogs should be kept permanently on your right. This keeps you as the owner in the blocking position, creating a buffer between the trail user and your dog.

Like Rock, Scissors, Paper, dogs on trails should always defer to any and every other trail user. Scissor beats paper, rock beats scissor, paper beats rock? Hikers, walkers, bicyclists, runners, roller-bladers, skateboarders, cross-country skiers always beat dogs.

The best way to manage your dog on the trail and to create good trail manners in your dog is to teach him to ignore all other trail users, dogs and people.

We love our trails. We love being able to take our dogs on these trails. We love having the open space in which we can be outdoors with our dogs. We want to remain welcome on our trails and in the woods. In order to keep our communities happy and welcoming/inviting to our dogs, the following is a list of suggestions for simple trail etiquette:

No matter how well-behaved you know or believe your dog to be, dogs should always be maneuvered off the trail or a least to the far/opposite side of you/of the oncoming trail user. The handler should always be in the blocking position, or in the middle of the dog-trail-user-sandwich.

MOVE OFF THE TRAIL:

Whenever another dog comes along the trail, MOVE OFF THE TRAIL.

Whenever another trail user hikes by, MOVE OFF THE TRAIL.

Whenever a bicyclist rides past, MOVE OFF THE TRAIL.

Other trail users don't know that your dog is friendly (hopefully he is…) and shouldn't need to worry and wonder if your dog will lunge or jump up at them as they get within range. As dog owning trail users, we should have to work extra hard at keeping dogs welcome on our trails by behaving politely and going out of our way to accommodate and respect all other trail users. We can't just exist on the trails as dog owners; we have to shine, to impress other trail users with exemplary manners.

TIPS:

Trish King, of the Marin Humane Society in Novato, California, recommends responsible owners carry a quick-release umbrella. When there is an incoming off–leash dog, and your own dog is iffy with other dogs (or your own dog is tiny, and the approaching dog is huge…) you simply pop open the umbrella, which simultaneously acts as a shield around your dog and a surprising deterrent for the approaching dog. Trish is a brilliant dog trainer and has many such clever and creative solutions for common problems.

CHAPTER THREE

CONTROLLING YOUR DOG DURING PLAY

IF YOU OWN MORE THAN ONE DOG

Getting control of your own dog around other dogs often needs to start right in your own home. Do you have more than one dog? Do they play together? Then training each of your own dogs, separately, to respond instantly to you, even while they're engaged in play, starts at home. Very often, dogs who have playmates at home with whom they play obsessively, are out of control in the presence of other dogs.

Your goal is to have your dog(s) leave his play partner and come over to you when you call him. The real goal is to make sure you maintain control over your dog, even when he's excited. Remember, it's not healthy or safe for a dog to consider another dog more fun than a human, particularly you—his owner!

Begin indoors, in the comfort of your own home.

LURING:

• Pick one of your dogs to begin the training. Train each dog separately.

• Use high value food treats—tiny, very high value, soft (no time wasted chewing) yummy treats.

• Go directly to his nose with treats in both hands.

• Once he catches a whiff, step backwards about 3 or 4 steps, and bring your hands to your belt buckle. Keeping your hands together and touching your own body will ensure that your dog comes straight and close enough to you (using one hand to feed the treats trains a dog to come in and list to that side, often getting more and more crooked when he arrives).

TIPS:

You want your dog close to you when he comes so that in the case of an emergency, he is always close enough for you to grab his collar. If you lean over, reach out to feed food treats, your dog will tend to sit further and further away from you, and you won't be able to reach him.

WHEN YOUR DOG GETS TO YOU:

• As soon as your dog reaches you and touches your hands, praise him profusely, feed him one treat from one hand, and then another treat from the other hand, then ask him to sit, and when he does, feed him another treat from the other hand.

• After he sits, keep him sitting while you feed him one treat from each hand, one after the other, switching hands each time for at least 15 seconds.

• Before you run out of treats, shoo your dog away and turn your back on the dog and ignore him for at least a few minutes. You are trying to disengage him from the training so you can repeat another training sequence.

TIPS:

What you don't want is for your dog to learn that coming means tagging you, getting just one predictable treat and then running away to do his own thing. You want to teach your dog to come to you, even when he's having fun with his friends, sit in front of you for a period of time long enough for him to calm down before you release him with an 'okay' and shoo him to go back and play.

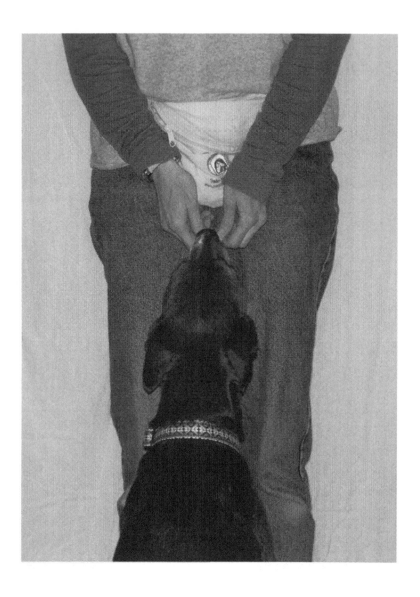

NEXT TRAINING STEPS

ADDING A NAME FOR THE BEHAVIOR:

Then add on a 'recall' label, or command, to the training. "Come" or "Here" work well.

*Start with your dog somewhere else besides right in front of you.

*Using his name first, call out the command, 'Come!', and step backwards about 2–3 steps.

*Carry your treats in both hands.

*Keep both your hands in front of you to lure your dog into the sit-front attention position you've previously worked on.

Then repeat the above sequence but *start the training by interrupting your dogs while they are actively engaged in play.*

LURING:

• *Wait until your dogs are actively engaged in play. Choose one dog to train at a time.*

• *Use high value food treats—tiny, very high value, soft (no time wasted chewing) yummy treats.*

• *Go directly to one dog's nose with treats in both hands.*

• *Once he catches a whiff, step backwards about 3 or 4 steps, and bring your hands to your belt buckle. Keeping your hands together and touching your own body will ensure that your dog comes in straight and close enough to you (using one hand to feed the treats trains a dog to come in and list to that side, often getting more and more crooked when he arrives).*

SECTION TWO

Introduction

For many dogs, group dog play can offer hours of socializing, exercise, mental stimulation and fun.

For many owners who work full time and own young, active dogs, group dog play can mean the difference between having a dog or not having a dog, since the dog park allows busy working owners easy access to off-leash play time and exercise—and hence a tired living companion at the end of a long day. At its best, dog-to-dog playtime can be entertaining and heartwarming. It can be great, tiring, aerobic exercise. It can be fun and stimulating and time for inter-species socialization.

At its worst, dog-to-dog playtime can mean rehearsal for serious aggression, trauma (both emotional and physical), injury or, in rare cases, death. Some dogs are well cut out for dog-to-dog play. They enjoy play, they play well, and they reap the many benefits. But some dogs are not cut out for dog-to-dog play. These dogs can spark fights, cause friction, intimidate, threaten and sometimes injure other dogs. Some dogs are just plain miserable when participating in group dog situations, finding them very stressful.

More and more urban areas have their own Dog Parks or Dog Runs—designated fenced-in areas just for dogs to have off-leash freedom. In many urban areas, these fenced-in Dog Parks are the only legal available off-leash territories. Without appropriate dog–to–dog play skills, many

urban dogs will have no opportunity for off–leash exercise whatsoever.
Dog Parks tend to have a low risk of harm compared to the benefits
of socializing and exercising. However, there are also many Dog Parks
filled with frighteningly dangerous dog-to-dog encounters, and daily
reports of bites, not only to dogs but to humans as well. Yes, daily.

As a dog trainer, watching the activities at any given Dog Park can be
a terrifying experience. I squirm when I watch some of the dogs interacting. While most encounters do not end in mishap, the number of
near-miss dangerous interactions is too many for me to relax and enjoy
watching.

This section is designed to provide you with the knowledge that will
help you observe the details and often subtle warning signs of when a
dog-to-dog encounter might turn sour and end up in a fight. This section encourages you to become an active partner in your dog's playtime.
Instead of just spectating and relying on luck for the safety and enjoy-
ment of your dog, this section can give you concrete behaviors to look for,
suggestions for when to intervene on your dog's behalf, and when to take
your dog out of the park.

CHAPTER ONE
Understanding Dog Play

PART ONE: WHAT IS HEALTHY PLAY?

What does healthy play look like? The following are some of the elements that can identify normal and appropriate play between dogs.

1. Acceptable Roles

One dog may start out on top of the other (literally) and may be the one to initiate most of the rules and moves, but the roles should be acceptable to both dogs, and the air space and physical contact between them should be shared.

2. Intensity Rises and Falls on Its Own

Normal play arousal levels should remain low to moderate. Play that arouses to an intense level, or spikes suddenly in arousal levels, can detonate a fight. Intensity of play that rises and falls on its own, without a squabble or human intervention to diffuse the situation, is an indicator of good, healthy play. Healthy play self-interrupts.

3. Similar Play Styles with Mimicking

Some dogs enjoy mouth wrestling, some enjoy a good game of chase, some enjoy poking and play bowing, every dog has a particular style of play he is most comfortable with, and finding a matching partner in style and energy is usually a recipe for healthy playtime. Dogs engaged in healthy play will often mimic each other, both while playing and while resting. They may face the same direction, strike the same poses, sniff the same object, etc.

4. Shared and Respected Physical Space

What does this mean? Like dance partners, good playmates share their physical space and push neither too hard nor too often at each other. If one dog is clearly pounding and driving the other dog(s) out of his physical space, this signals a serious imbalance. Healthy play is physically compatible—each dog moving in and out of the shared space between them with gentle to moderate and equal physical contact.

5. Relaxed Bodies

Dogs should look basically relaxed during play—their bodies should be "blobs" at least half the time—blobs on the ground, blobs draped over the other dog, rolling blobs. Dogs who play stiffly, and hard, tense and taut may not be playing. In true, relaxed play, a dog's head and spine should not remain in one single straight line, nor be rigid like ironing boards. The dogs' spines should be curved and bend and twist during play, with their heads off-set. While dogs can show excitement and arousal during play, both partners should appear relaxed in between bouts of more aroused play.

6. Play Should Be Fun

How can you tell if your dog is having fun? Break the dogs apart, and then let go—dogs who are having fun will both want to go back and have more fun. If only one dog wants to go back, chances are the other dog wasn't having as much fun. Also, dogs should start anticipating arrival at the dog park and look excited and eager to be there: tails up, pulling somewhat (hopefully not completely out of control...) to get into the Dog Park.

PART TWO: WHAT IS UNHEALTHY PLAY?
What does inappropriate and unhealthy play look like?

1. Lopsided Interactions—One Dog is Intense and Out of Control

One dog might be pursuing another dog relentlessly, and spending more than half of the play session chasing, grabbing, mounting, pummeling, muzzle-punching, pushing and shoving at another dog.

2. Escalating Arousal Levels

Watch for play that may start out well, but gets more and more intense, the arousal levels climbing higher and higher without any breaks occurring naturally (or without human interruption).

3. Disparate Play Styles

Watch for incompatible play styles. Some dogs may prefer lolling mouth wrestling, one dog lying on the ground while another dogs lolls over him and they mouth wrestle together. Some dogs prefer a hard-driving, fairly physical style of action-play, and this more physical style can easily intimidate, scare or hurt more sensitive dogs. Fights can often erupt when a hard—driving, strong, physical dog initiates play by pummeling the other dog, and the dog receiving the pummeling is both surprised and a little hurt, and responds by yelping or a quick defensive display (teeth bared, snarling, etc.) The strong–but–relatively–innocent dog then wonders why this other dog that he just tried to initiate play with is so grouchy and aggressive, and may respond by aggressing back. All of that may be a misunderstanding due to incompatible play-styles.

4. Bullying or Ganging Up

Watch out for physical space that is claimed by one dog more than another. If one dog is constantly and consistently pushing, invading, chest-thrusting, body-slamming, hip-checking another dog, (especially if TWO dogs are doing this and ganging up on another dog) this is a sign that the play is out of balance, and probably not fun for the dog receiving this attention.

5. Dogs Who are Stiff and Tense

Dogs who are rigid, or stiff-legged and stiff-tailed when perusing the Dog Park, and maintain this posture while greeting or passing more than half of the other dogs, are 'testy', and are probably not having fun, nor are the other dogs around him. Even though these stiff and tense-type dogs may not actively be causing harm, they may feel they have too much at stake, or too much status to maintain, or too much rank to show off to be able to relax and enjoy the Dog Park. They are usually pretty edgy and close to fighting, since they are rarely relaxed and enjoying themselves and those around them.

6. Targeting Behavior

"Targeting" behavior is when a dog chooses one particular dog and focuses all his attention and energy onto that one dog. A dog may target another dog and spend most of his time pursuing and following this particular dog. The dog that has targeted another dog often tracks the other dog with his own ears up and pricked forward, may get sexually aroused by the dog he has chosen to target, and end up humping, mounting, or nose-bopping onto the back of his target. Even if the dog that is targeting another dog looks like he wants to play, it doesn't matter. Obsessive behavior, whether it's obsessed with playing or obsessed with fighting, isn't healthy.

7. Predatory Behaviors

Watch out for play that is comprised of deep-mouthed grabbing—where one dog has the other dog deep in the back of his mouth, especially when this is accompanied by head-shaking, thrashing back and forth, or strong tugging of the other dog. Watch out for repeated grabbing or targeting (with the mouth) another dog's belly, armpits, or the back of his neck. Play biting that looks like it hurts the other dog probably does.

8. Constant Arousal and Intensity

An unrelenting state of arousal from any one dog is a red flag. High arousal is indicated by a dog's ears constantly pricked forward, his brow furrowed (scowling), his eyes large and round, an arched or tense neck, and a continuous eye-head-spine alignment when interacting with another dog. High arousal levels keep a dog close to aggression, and a constant state of high arousal can be a time bomb.

43

CHAPTER TWO:

Identifying The Cast Of Characters at the Dog Park

Every dog has his own particular play style. Some dogs have more than one play style they use when interacting with another dog, depending on the personality of that particular dog. These play 'chameleons' are often well suited to the Dog Park. Listed below are the most likely cast of characters to be found at any public Dog Park, along with the most compatible and most risky playmate styles. Do any match your own dog?

(In alphabetical order...)

The Bully

The Bully is a very common player in the Dog Park, because Bullies usually love to 'play'; the problem is that most of the Bully's playmates are NOT loving it quite as much as the Bully. The Bully tends to play in a relentless and very physical style. The Bully uses his size, his strength and his persistence to overcome his playmates. The Bully's play is very one-sided. Bully dogs often grow up as bullies—and if they live in a household with another dog (or dogs) who put up with their bullying, they may become even worse Bullies. Since most Bullies look like they're playing and having fun (they are…), owners of Bullies tend not to acknowledge just how unpleasant their dogs can be. The dogs who interact with Bullies are aware that the Bully is a bully, and are usually trying to get away or playing very defensively and are usually not having fun.

Compatible Playmates for The Bully

The only dog who should be playing with a Bully is a strong, physically capable dog who likes playing on the defensive, is more agile than the Bully, can squirt himself out of the way and antagonize the Bully back by moving so quickly and intensely that he keeps from being battered. Owners of Bullies should take great care to call their Bully off play at least once every few minutes or more, and only allow their dog back to play if the playmate approaches the Bully and initiates play. Otherwise, it's simply Bullying and that's not okay.

Risky Playmates for The Bully

Almost all other playmates are risky for the Bully—though the Bully (and often his owner) will be unaware of this. Play, by its very definition, should be reciprocal and balanced, and bullying rarely allows for this. The most risky playmates are physically fragile dogs, small dogs, or dogs who get intimidated easily and respond on the defensive with aggression. This can cause a fight to break out, since the Bully will not understand why his playmate got aggressive, and he himself may respond back with aggression.

Also, Bullying is usually relentless and intense. Without frequent inter-ruption and intervention from the Bully's owner, Bully play can arouse to a point which could break out into a serious fight.

Most Bullies really do not belong in the dog park. In order for the Bully to play well, he needs a very narrow range of play partners. Finding the right partner at any given time at the Dog Park is rare. The greatest risk for bullies is that they get out of control in play, and hence out of control in other parts of their lives.

The Chaser

The Chaser loves to chase other dogs, or loves to be chased. Chasers are quite common, and chasing is probably the most common type of play in dogs. It is also great aerobic exercise. Some dogs will go to any length to get another dog to chase them, while others want only to chase another dog. Other dogs will take the game in either direction.

Chase is best played with only a couple of dogs, as a game of chase will often attract, like magnets, other dogs to join in on the chase, which can ignite into a mob attack onto the dog being chased. Chasing is exciting enough to arouse even the calmest dog to join the posse. Caution: many a flank has been ripped open by the joyous 'nipping' of the over-the-top chaser.

Chase also runs the risk of quickly triggering into an out-of-control game. A game of chase can escalate, in an instant, into a pack of wild, uncontrol-lable beasts, and all the screaming and yelling and calling for your dog fall onto deaf ears. It is dangerous for any game to escalate out of control, especially high–speed games, like chase.

Compatible Playmates for The Chaser

Obviously, the best playmates for dogs who like to be chased are dogs who want to chase. The best playmates for dogs who enjoy chasing, are dogs who like to be chased. There should be a similarity in size and bulk and how physically invasive they are toward the other dog(s).

Risky Playmates for The Chaser

The riskiest playmates for a dog who loves to chase are ones that don't wish to be chased. How can you tell? The dog being chased might have his tail tucked most of the time during the chase. The dog being chased might not have any chance to rest, because if he stops or slows to even change direction, the Chaser rolls him, hip-checks him, runs him over, or clobbers him physically, mentally, or behaviorally.

The riskiest situation for the Chaser is the environment in which the chase actually erupts. If there are other dogs who get caught up in the posse and the game becomes a real predatory attack, it is no longer a game. On the other hand, if the chase takes place in an environment with just a few dogs, or dogs that don't join in, or in ample space, or on a challenging surface that prohibits speed (like sand or deep gravel), then chase is a great game.

More important than with almost any other type of play, chase games should be frequently interrupted and absolute verbal control and supervision should accompany every game of chase.

The Grouch

The Grouch is the dog who walks rather slowly around the Dog Park, actually exercising very little, tail usually raised up, forehead usually furrowed from a permanent scowl, grumping, growling, posturing at every opportunity. The Grouch often minds his or her own business, but when approached, the Grouch is usually snarky: growling, hair up, maybe a mild lunge forward before scoffing away. The Grouch almost never plays, and if he does, it's ever so briefly, and only with a very persistent and jolly dog. The Grouch may ignite fights every so often, particularly when the territory already has one resident Grouch, as two Grouches usually provoke a fight. Grouches spend most of their time in the Dog Park sniffing, urinating, walking, standing, bristling. Many times the Grouch can be found hovering near the entrance to the play yard, as it is there that the Grouch can immediately establish and warn the incoming dog (while that incoming dog is still new and unsettled) that there is a Grouch present and requiring respect.

Compatible Playmates for The Grouch

While serious fights are rare, the Grouch is a testy dog, and really has little desire to play. There are no real compatible playmates for the Grouch, because I don't believe the Grouch wants to play, enjoys play, or should be forced to play. While I observe a lot of Grouches in dog play yards that are relatively benign, that is their best behavior. At worst, they intimidate and can spark fights. I don't believe it is in the best interest of the Grouch to engage in group-play with other dogs. The Grouches I see in Dog Parks are 'getting by', not enjoying themselves, not adding to the fun of others, nor are they exercising in any meaningful way.

Really, Grouches should be taken for solo walks around the neighborhood, where they can enjoy good sniffing, urine-marking territory, strutting past other dogs, and get some much needed one-on-one attention from their owners.

Risky Playmates for The Grouch

'Playmate' is not an appropriate term for the Grouch, since Grouches really don't want to play, and usually won't play. Almost every other dog encountered in a group play yard is at risk from the Grouch. The least risky dogs to be with a Grouch would be dogs that completely ignore other dogs and have no desire for status whatsoever.

The Humper

Male or female, neutered or intact, it doesn't matter—the Humper just loves to hump other dogs. Humping (or mounting) is usually not sexually based, but rather a dominance display. Sometimes humping is just part of getting over-stimulated around other dogs, and the arousal leads to humping. Not all dogs enjoy being humped. Other dogs ride around with the Humper on their back, going about his routine as if no one were aboard. The Humper will even 'air' hump if the dog he's humping pulls out.

Compatible Playmates for The Humper

Any dog that doesn't mind or seem to notice being "ridden", or humped, or mounted, is a compatible playmate for the Humper. However, the Humper's owner should interrupt this behavior frequently, as it seems to increase in frequency and intensity the more the Humper is allowed to persist. Other dogs that make good playmates for the Humper are dogs that will not tolerate being humped, dogs that immediately turn around and discipline the Humper, as long as the Humper accepts and discipline and doesn't fight back.

Risky Playmates for The Humper

Riskiest playmates for the Humper are dogs that get upset, anxious or aggressive when being humped. The most risky playmates are not necessarily ones that will fight with the Humper, but rather those that are miserable when being relentlessly humped. Again, it is the responsibility of the Humper's owner to come to the rescue of any dog the Humper is relentlessly humping, and call their Humper off and away.

The Hunter-Seeker

The Hunter-Seeker is the dog that chooses one dog and pursues it. The Hunter-Seeker selects one victim and follows that dog around consistently. The Hunter-Seeker may never follow through and do anything to or with his chosen target, but he will stare at, pursue, follow, and act out an obsession with this chosen dog. The Hunter-Seeker may occasionally poke at, jab with his nose, mount, and place his chin over the shoulders of his chosen target.

What does this behavior mean? This can be risky behavior between dogs. Some dogs engage pretty exclusively in Hunter-Seeker behaviors, and even though no serious incident may have ever occurred, the behavior can develop into something dangerous, as it has all the components of high-risk dog-to-dog interaction: relentless, obsessive, predatory, difficult-to-interrupt.

Whether your dog is the Hunter-Seeker or the hunted target, neither dog should be allowed to continue in this type of behavior. In general, if you own

The Hunter-Seeker, you'll want to explore and identify ways to exercise your dog other than at the Dog Park, and other than interacting with other dogs. If your dog is the target of a Hunter-Seeker, you'll want to call your own dog to you and leave the situation until the Hunter-Seeker has left the park.

Compatible Playmates for The Hunter–Seeker

The only compatible playmate for the Hunter-Seeker would be a dog that the Hunter-Seeker does not engage in hunting-seeking behaviors with. This may be a strange dog at a public Dog Park, or it may be the one dog that the Hunter-Seeker lives with.

A harmless partner for the Hunter-Seeker is a very benign, placid, low-key dog that is considerably larger than the Hunter-Seeker and at no risk of being injured should the Hunter-Seeker decide to follow-through with violence. This partner should have a well-known history free of any aggressive dog-to-dog interactions.

Risky Playmates for The Hunter–Seeker

Almost everyone the Hunter-Seeker targets is at risk. The behavior itself is not play. It is an obsessive part of a predatory sequence and it is unsafe to let the dog practice this. Even with a history of no harm done, the behavior should not be taken lightly or allowed to repeat itself.

The "Kick-Me" Dog

There seem to be dogs born with a "Kick-Me" sign, and wherever they go, other dogs seem to target them, attack them, scare them, or bowl them over. People who own the "Kick-Me" dog know exactly what I'm describing. Their dog seems to offer no instigating or provocative behaviors, and yet, in so many instances, other dogs, even those with no history of problems with other dogs, will seek out and attack the "Kick-Me" dog. My guess is that the "Kick-Me" dog is giving off some sort of mixed signal, or some sort of antagonizing cue, whether he is aware of it or not, that sets other dogs off and causes them to pick on him.

51

Compatible Playmates for The Kick–Me Dog

Most "Kick-Me" dogs are attacked at the very start of an interaction, and not well into a play session. So, any dog that the "Kick-Me" dog is already playing with should be a safe playmate. If you have the type of "Kick-Me" dog that has a history of being attacked in the middle of a play session, then I would avoid play with unknown dogs at all times, and if your dog has a few familiar, long-term, safe, good friends, let your dog play only with those friends; otherwise, avoid play with any other dog(s). Just to be on the safe side. The Dog Park is an unsafe place to take the "Kick-Me" dog, and an unfair place as well. Your dog needs to know you'll do everything in your power, at all times, to keep your dog safe. And if he wears a "Kick-Me" sign, off leash group dog play is hazardous.

Risky Playmates for The Kick–Me Dog

A risky playmate is any dog significantly larger or stronger than the "Kick-Me" dog, and any dog that hones in on the "Kick-Me" dog immediately: any dog that starts staring at your "Kick-Me" dog upon entering the visual range of the dog is a risk.

Any dog with a history of "sometimes not liking other dogs" is particularly risky for interaction with the "Kick-Me" dog, since he is all too likely to "not like" this playmate.

The Misfit

The Misfit is the dog that just doesn't seem to mesh with most other dogs. The Misfit might be a grouch, or stand-off-ish with the other dogs. The Misfit is, in general, not a dog that is either skilled at, or enjoys playing with other dogs. The Misfit is often the canine nerd, the dog not well socialized or just plain uncomfortable with other dogs. Sometimes the Misfit is unpopular, and gets ignored, or the Misfit ignores other dogs.

Often, the Misfit is an older, ornery dog that peruses the dog park, sniffing, peeing, posturing when he meets other dogs; he may growl a lot, he may put the hair up on his back frequently, his ears may be forward most of the time, and he may carry with him a scowl—a furrowed brow. The Misfit rarely PLAYS in any joyful manner, mostly he crabs and maneuvers around the dog park by himself.

Compatible Playmates for The Misfit

Consider exercising the Misfit in places other than the Dog Park. Because the Misfit rarely actually engages in play, and rarely actually EXERCISES— he may benefit more from a brisk half hour or longer walk with his owner, stopping occasionally to sniff and mark new territories, new parking meters, passing new dogs, but not actually stopping to greet dogs. The Misfit would probably prefer to explore new territories each day, and sniff and pee on new and different traffic light stanchions than visit the dog park, and have to behaviorally and physically maneuver around so many dogs in such a small area.

Risky Playmates for The Misfit

While the Misfit may not pose much of a danger to other dogs, he is at some risk to himself if he grouches or postures with the wrong dog. The Misfit sometimes doesn't back down from a fight, and tends to provoke tension with his lack of submissive and/or play postures, so if the Misfit meets up with the wrong dog—a dog that is large and truly aggressive—he may start a fight he cannot win.

The Pest

The Pest is a common player in almost any dog playgroup. The Pest is often gregarious and persistent, mingling among most of the other dogs, relentlessly trying to engage every other dog in play, or sometimes, not-so-much-play. Sometimes the Pest doesn't care so much whether the other dogs actually want to play, and is just as happy if he annoys the other dog(s) into growling, snarling or going after him. Pests often like to create a stir—and they thrive on any kind of interaction with other dogs, and will relish a good snark as much as a good game.

The Pest is sometimes out of control when it comes to being around other dogs, and can start spiraling more and more out of control the closer he gets to the Dog Park. Owners of Pesty dogs usually aren't aware that they own a Pest. Owners of the dogs that the Pesty Dog pesters are usually quite aware that there is a Pesty dog pestering their dog.

Compatible Playmates for The Pest

The best playmates for the Pest are very insensitive, raucous players. However, the fallout of compatible playmates for the Pest is that the more tolerant the playmate, the more encouraging it is for the Pest to be even pestier. And while a Pest rarely develops into a true monster, it is not the type of behavior you necessarily want to encourage in your dog, since it is out-of-control behavior.

Risky Playmates for The Pest

The riskiest playmates are ones who respond to the relentless and insensitive pursuits of the Pest with aggressive displays, as The Pest could then return in kind with aggression, not understanding the apparent unprovoked grouchiness from the playmate. Equally as risky are playmates who cannot defend themselves and end up on the defensive and unhappy. It is unfair to allow a Pest to relentlessly take advantage of other dogs who cannot seem to defend or take care of themselves. It is worthwhile to reiterate that Pests need to be controlled and heavily monitored if and when playing with other dogs. Pests should not be allowed unsupervised play with any other dogs, including dogs they live with, since it encourages the Pest to not listen or respect the owner, and can lead to control problems in other areas of life. At its worst, in younger dogs (under two years of age) uninterrupted play can cause the Pest to develop into an aggressive dog, since the line between over-aroused play and fighting is so fine.

The Play Police Officer

In almost any play group there is a dog that patrols the area, cutting in an cutting off any type of play he deems illegal for that moment. The Play Police Officer can be a male or a female, although more often than not, Pl Police Officers seem to be bitches! Play Police Officers have very particula interpretations of the law, and may respond to many different types of play. Very often, the Play Police Officer steps in and stops rough play, and will stop play that is quickly escalating in intensity. The Play Police Officer is ver often an older dog, a deeply opinionated older dog, and one that is pretty intolerant of any excitable or fast moving play. Sometimes, the Play Police Officer can be quite a party pooper, and may not be the most welcome or appropriate dog in a group setting.

Compatible Playmates for The Play Police Officer

The Play Police Officer seldom actually wants to play with other dogs, and finding a compatible playmate usually means finding other dogs that aren't playing, or other dogs that aren't doing much at all.

Every once in a while, a Play Police Officer fits well with one particular dog, and will actually initiate or acquiesce in play, and if that happens, then that is the one compatible playmate.

Risky Playmates for The Play Police Officer

At risk from the Play Police Officer are any dogs that are playing. They might be chasing, or mouth–wrestling, or play–bowing—it could be any behavior that sets off the Play Police Officer and stops the fun.

In general, higher–ranking, or high–status–seeking dogs will not appreciat being interrupted or 'corrected' by the Play Police Officer, and could even fight back when interrupted.

On the other hand, in the absence of owners who do any of their own policing, a canine Play Police Officer is probably better than no police enforcement at all!

The Pummeler

The Pummeler is a physical, invasive, fairly relentless player, who plays by invading the other dog's space repeatedly, and keeps his playmates on the defensive. The Pummeler often uses his front paws to swipe at or lead the rest of his body as he rears up like a bear and goes at the other dogs. The Pummeler should be well supervised by his owners, and interrupted frequently. The Pummeler should not be allowed to play at all with other dogs until and unless the owners can easily call him off of another dog and keep him at attention for at least 30 seconds. The Pummeler should be interrupted frequently and asked to rest, regain attention towards humans, and lower his arousal levels before being given permission to go back and play.

Compatible Playmates for The Pummeler

The Pummeler often rides the line between play and aggression, and needs very hardy, very experienced partners, dogs with confidence and either physical substance or athletic ability that compares with the Pummeler. The Pummeler's best playmates are often those that enjoy being chased, or the thrill of being on the defensive.

Risky Playmates for The Pummeler

The Pummeler not only needs specific playmates, but also should be well-supervised during all his interactions. The most risky playmates are dogs that arouse easily, or frighten or freak out easily. Dogs who enjoy being chased can make good playmates, but if The Pummeler starts a high-speed game of chase, he should be called off immediately and the chase not allowed. Pummelers play well with other Pummelers. Orthopedically fragile dogs may be at higher risk of harm than physically sound playmates. Dogs with protruding eyes at risk of corneal scratches are risky playmates for Pummelers.

The Puppy

For Puppies six months and younger, very special care should be taken to build good, fun, healthy play. The more positive play experiences The Puppy has during his first six months will not only build healthy play skills, but can also act as a buffer should a traumatic experience occur. Puppies with few positive experiences with other dogs are more likely to remember one bad experience and have it affect them permanently.

While Puppies are in part born with certain temperament qualities that determine how well (or not) they will interact and play with other dogs, socialization, or the act of creating a series of positive and healthy interactions with other dogs, can greatly increase the odds of raising a Puppy that grows into an adult with adequate to good dog-dog skills.

There are Puppies, however, who, despite many positive play experiences, grow up not getting along well with other dogs, and some Puppies, despite positive play experiences, grow up aggressive with other dogs. In itself, this isn't the worst behavior or temperament problem to have. Aggression towards other dogs, or an inability to get along well with lots of unfamiliar dogs, such as in a Dog Park, isn't the worst diagnosis for a dog. In order to live a successful, happy, and fulfilling life, a dog can skip going to a Dog Park altogether, and find alternative ways to exercise. All a good dog has to be able to do to be a truly good dog is to ignore other dogs while on leash. He never HAS TO stop and meet them successfully. That can be avoided.

Compatible Playmates for The Puppy

The most compatible playmates for the Puppy would be a mixture of other puppies the same age that play in a similar fashion, or experienced adult dogs that give off clear signals for when it's time to play, when it's time to stop playing, and are able to communicate, effectively and instantly, when the Puppy is being intrusive, invasive, inappropriate or too bold. A Puppy should not just play with other Puppies, but needs as much experience with benevolent but firm adult dogs—adults that can set clear limits.

Risky Playmates for The Puppy

The riskiest playmates for Puppies would include Bullies, or physically pushy and invasive dogs that ignore signals from their playmates to stop. Puppies should be protected from intimidation, whether the intimidation is physical brutality or emotional intimidation from subtly aggressive play partners.

Risky playmates also include other dogs of any age that are TOO compatible, and owners who don't frequently interrupt and reward their puppies for attention to humans. Too much play can be as risky as inappropriate play in regards to Puppy development. Puppies that enjoy play too much, and feel that the sight of another dog is an invitation to play, grow into adolescent dogs who are out of control at the sight of another dog. This can lead to excessive frustration at the sight of another dog and lead to barrier (on-leash) aggression or aggressive displays.

The Small Dog

Small dogs are defined as any dog weighing 20 pounds and under, excluding most Jack Russell terriers and other terriers. Small dogs need special consideration since their diminutive size and fragility put them at greater risk of harm from most larger dogs. Since healthy play is very reliant on respect for air space and physical boundaries, size disparities between large dogs and small dogs can make for play that is, at best, defensive from the small dogs, and at worst, a predatory sequence where the small dog's life is truly at stake.

Compatible Playmates for The Small Dog

Other similarly sized dogs are the best choice for small dogs. Some large dogs will lie down and modify how they play and tone down both their size and intensity when playing with small dogs. These are excellent choices for the toy guys. Always supervise play between toy dogs and large dogs. There is too much opportunity for damage for people to get complacent.

Often, a fearful, sensitive and agile dog can make a good playmate for a highly playful toy dog, since the fearful dog often skirts away from actual physical contact, and having a small but confident companion to feel comfortable around other dogs can benefit both dogs.

Risky Playmates for The Small Dog

The riskiest playmates are any dogs that are physically capable of harming the toy dog. That would include muscular, athletic dogs even a few pounds larger than their toy dog playmates. Small terriers with lots of prey-chase-hunting instincts are equally as risky for toy dogs. Care and proactive supervision must always be taken when allowing toy dogs to play with anything but other toy dogs.

The Smoosher

The Smoosher is the dog, usually a larger sized dog, that plays very much with his front end, and often mashes his chest into another dog, or swats at the other dog with his front paws, pushing into that dog's space; also, the smoosher often rolls onto the other dog while they are wrestling.

Compatible Playmates for The Smoosher

Good playmates for the Smoosher include hardy small or medium lithe, athletic dogs, who shoot out of the way and enjoy the challenge of staying out of the way; other compatible playmates can include other smooshers, or physical dogs that move slowly and don't mind the hard physical contact.

Risky Playmates for The Smoosher

Special concern should be taken for small fragile or toy dogs, which risk injury to them if they land underneath the Smoosher. Also a risk are dogs of any size who are sensitive to body contact, and might react defensively if they are the recipient of The Smoosher's weight.

CHAPTER THREE:

Assessing Your Dog Before Going to the Dog Park

Young dogs (under a year and a half) generally like to play, and generally get along well with many other dogs. As they get older, many dogs enjoy playing less, or they enjoy playing with a few familiar friends, but lose the patience to meet and greet lots of new friends, and tend to get grumpier or grouchier with dogs as they mature. It is not unusual for a dog to mature into a dog that doesn't get along well with other dogs in a play group. He certainly shouldn't be in a play group, but just because he can't get along in that setting doesn't necessarily mean he is a "bad" dog or an "aggressive" dog, or somehow dysfunctional.

A good dog merely has to tolerate, ignore, or mind his own business when encountering other dogs, and as long as your dog isn't a heat-seeking missile intent on injuring another dog, your dog can be a great canine citizen. You'll just have to find ways) of exercising him other than taking him to a dog-dog play group.

Remember, there is nothing wrong with you or your dog if your dog doesn't want to go to the Dog Park.

1. Does your dog weigh less than 20 pounds?

Yes [ ]   No [ ]

Small dogs, in particular dogs less than 20 pounds, should play only with like-sized dogs, unless the dog skills and behavior of the larger dog are well–known. Many larger dogs, especially when aroused or in a group (more than one) of dogs, will consider small dogs as prey. It is not uncommon for a high-speed game of chase to ignite into a predatory pack hunt with injuries to the targeted dog. The risk of serious injury or even death to small dogs in a mixed play group is too great. There is no room for error.

One-on-one play between a gentle, appropriate larger dog and a smaller dog is fine, but larger play groups, particularly when made up of unknown dogs, should be avoided. Do not wait for a problem. Don't mix sizes.

Some terriers under 20 pounds are robust, physical, tough little dogs and may be safe playing with appropriate larger dogs. Many of these same terrier type dogs may also look at smaller, lightweight dogs as prey and may not be so safe with them.

2. Is your dog younger than seven months of age?

Yes [ ]   No [ ]

The younger your dog is, the more vulnerable both behaviorally and physically. A traumatic event for a dog younger than seven months can potentially have a more lasting ill effect than the same single traumatic event for a more mature and experienced dog. It is therefore important to be extra-protective of younger dogs, and pick their play partners carefully.

Younger dogs have fewer "good and fun" experiences to fall back on in case of a fright, so the ratio of good experiences to frightful experiences is smaller, making those frightful events that much more memorable.

On the other hand, it is a good idea for puppies to play with appropriate adult dogs, instead of just playing with other puppies. In fact, playing only with other puppies can sometimes serve to exaggerate each puppy's doggie interactive flaws, and make a bully more of a bully, and make the shy pup even shyer.

It's wise to be extra careful and vigilant when bringing puppies six months and under into a group dog play situation.

If you are bringing your puppy to the Dog Park, remember to interrupt puppy play frequently, insert yourself into the play session and call your puppy away from the other dogs and towards you. Have treats with you if you need to, have him sit in front of you paying attention to you and chill out for a few seconds, and then give him permission ("okay!") to go back and play. Puppies in particular need reminders that humans are in charge, humans are more fun than other dogs, and humans have control.

3. Have you recently adopted, rescued, found or acquired your dog, and his previous behavior around new dogs is unknown to you?

Yes [ ]   No [ ]

If you have recently adopted, rescued, found or acquired your dog, and his previous behavior history around new dogs is unknown or sketchy, you need to be especially vigilant the first time your new dog interacts with others. This is particularly so if your new dog is a large dog, or a muscular and athletic breed type, or a breed or breed mix whose original purpose was for fighting other dogs.

It can be hard to tell just how your dog might respond in an off–leash situation when he is leashed and frustrated. Often, just being on leash can cause a number of dogs to display aggression at oncoming dogs, but then these very same dogs play perfectly well when off–leash. Unfortunately, some dogs display aggression on–leash and also behave aggressively off–leash!

Before taking your unknown dog to a public Dog Park, try having him meet one or two safe, friendly, adult dogs. These may be dogs in your neighborhood, or dogs belonging to your friends. If they are meeting on-leash, make sure the leashes are loose when the dogs touch, and get ready to "maypole" around the two dogs as they circle and sniff. If the dogs are meeting off-leash, have a heavy jacket or clip-board or plant mister (set on "jet-stream") handy in case there is a squabble or an actual fight. Keep your attention on the dogs, and if you "feel" they are getting too aroused or a little out of control, they probably are, and you need to call your dog away and give him a rest.

If your new dog plays well with one or two safe and friendly dogs, then you can try bringing him to the Dog Park during a quiet time, when the park is pretty empty.

CHAPTER FOUR:

Assessing Your Dog's Behavior at the Dog Park

1. Does your dog get along with most new dogs, and spend at least 1/3 of his time at the Dog Park playing aerobically with other dogs, or running aerobically by himself or with a toy?

Yes [ ]   No [ ]

If you answered 'yes' to question #1, your dog sounds like a good candidate for the Dog Park. Continue with the test to make sure everything else is safe as well.

If you answered 'no' to question #1, continue on with the test.

2. Has your dog ever punctured or broken skin on another dog?

Yes [ ]   No [ ]

If you answered 'yes' to question #2, if the puncture or broken skin was on a dog from within your own household, and you answered 'yes' to question #1, your dog sounds like an okay candidate for the Dog Park. If the damage to the dog within your household was more than one puncture, or required a hospital visit, this may indicate a lack of inhibition in your dog, and could be a risk for other dogs in the Dog Park. In this case, your dog is NOT a safe candidate for the Dog Park.

If you answered 'yes' to question #2, and the puncture or broken skin was on a dog outside your household, even if you believe the fault lies with the other dog or owner, you need to think twice about bringing your dog to the Dog Park. Remember, the greatest predictor of future aggression is prior aggression. At the least, you may need to limit WHEN you go to the Dog Park, or WITH WHOM your dog plays. At the most, you may need to find other ways to exercise your dog and not bring your dog to the Dog Park. Your dog may be safest with a few good, familiar dog-friends, but should not go to a public Dog Park. If you choose to continue to take your dog to the Dog Park, understand your liability and responsibility to the other dogs and other dog owners. The owners of the other dogs, who may be the target of your dog's dislike, will appreciate your proactive approach.

If you answered 'no', your dog is likely a safe candidate for the Dog Park.

3. Has your dog ever punctured or broken skin on a human?

Yes [ ]   No [ ]

If your dog has bitten or punctured skin on a human, he does not belong in the Dog Park. Dogs with a bite history do not belong off leash in a public setting. Plain and simple. You may be able to control and modify your own behavior around your dog, and hence avoid a bite, but you will never be able to control the behavior of other people, and they will inevitably do whatever it is that will provoke your dog.

4. What is the frequency of squabbling (short bursts of growling, snapping, teeth-baring, mouths-open, etc.) between your dog and others?

0—1x per visit [ ]
1—3x per visit [ ]
4—10x per visit [ ]

Any more than the occasional squabble, which is 0–1x a visit, is too much. Playing in the Dog Park is all about meeting, greeting, getting along with, playing with other dogs, and aerobic exercise. Greetings are many, depending on how big and how many unfamiliar dogs your local Dog Park has. Squabbles indicate tense greetings. Squabbles are stressful for your own dog, and stressful for the other dog as well. Do your own dog a favor, as well as other dogs, by finding a different source of off–leash or aerobic exercise.

5. Does your dog squabble with almost every dog he meets, but it's over quickly and then he's fine?

Yes [ ]   No [ ]

If your dog squabbles with almost every dog he meets, even if he's "fine" directly afterwards, your dog does not belong in the Dog Park. This may not be what you want to hear, and you may think since no harm has been done that this is acceptable, but it really is not. And, it's really not fair for your dog. He most likely has a lot of status/rank issues, or a low-medium level aggressiveness with other dogs. This does not mean he is a bad dog—just a dog that shouldn't go into an off–leash group dog play situation.

6. Is your dog much stronger and does your dog play harder than most other dogs?

Yes [ ] No [ ]

If your dog is stronger or significantly more muscular than many other dogs, it is better to pick and choose specific play partners that are of equal strength, musculature, and moreover, enjoy playing hard and strong.

All too often, the dog who plays brutally really needs to find play partners who are just as brutal and enjoy the strong physical contact.

CHAPTER FIVE:
Identifying a Safe and Healthy Dog Park

? *What makes a good Dog Park? Here are a few elements to look for when deciding which Dog Park might be safe for your dog.*

Environment:

• Ample space. The larger the fenced in area, the better, but if it is a small space, look for a limited number of dogs. Crowding fuels fights and increases stress and tension.

• Separate areas within the larger space. This allows smaller social groups to form.

• A surface that requires the dogs to work hard to move—e.g. sand or gravel—keeps dogs from moving too fast and getting too much speed and over-stimulation, and condenses their exercise benefits.

• The fewer the human comforts (benches, etc), the better the interaction seems to be between owner and dog. The best Dog Parks may not be the most luxurious for the humans.

Humans:

• You should very quickly be able to match each dog to its owner. In other words, owners should be attentive and involved enough with their dogs so that you can easily tell who belongs to whom.

• Cell phones should be banned from Dog Parks! They distract owners. Only emergency calls should be allowed, and then the owner's dog should be leashed and taken out of the park for the duration of the call.

• Owners actively involved with their dogs indicate the best Dog Parks. Look for owners throwing balls, calling their dogs, petting their dogs, watching their dogs play, standing near their dogs.

• Annoying people aren't worth the stress. If there is someone you dislike or feel is irresponsible at the Dog Park, don't go, or go at another time.

Dogs:

• Dogs should be off leash and relaxed. If someone has a dog on leash, they are likely experiencing an aggression problem with that dog. Don't go in if another dog remains on leash.

• Look for dogs similar in size to your own. If the Dog Park is filled with big brutish dogs, and yours is smaller, or slighter, consider finding another Dog Park, or finding a time when more physically compatible dogs are present.

• It shouldn't matter why a dog is behaving badly—i.e. the dog was abused, or the dog was rescued from a traumatic situation, etc.—if the dog is behaving rudely or aggressively, find another Dog Park, or find another time to go.

• If many dogs linger about the entrance gate and pounce on the new arrivals, try to find another time to join. Entrances are difficult for dogs, and if there is a whole crew waiting to pounce on your dog...

• If there is one out of control dog that seems to be bothering all the other dogs, and the owner who is apathetic or just thinks his dog is 'fine', find another Dog Park or another time to go.

In Conclusion:

Few things in life are as entertaining and heartwarming as watching dogs play well together. Few things are as terrifying as witnessing a dogfight. While downright fun and an excellent source of exercise, playing with other dogs can also have its behavioral risks. Having to establish status anew with each unfamiliar dog can cause lots of anxiety to dogs for whom status is important. Other dogs who care less about status with unfamiliar dogs and will just play play play tend to have more fun.

Don't wait for a bite or a fight to help you realize that your dog was at risk, or, that your dog can cause harm. "Lack of event" is the way we seem to determine the success of most dog behavior situations regarding aggression. Using the "lack of event" to feel confident that things are safe, and that things are fine is not a good way of ensuring your dog's safety, happiness and well-being. Get in there and participate and intervene! If you are concerned or uncertain about an interaction between your dog and another, by all means go in and interrupt and give your dog a rest. No harm can be done by interrupting too much. Tremendous harm can be done if you don't intervene early enough.

CHAPTER SIX:
Dog Park Tips

Dog Park Tips

1.

Recognize that your dog may not get along with ALL other dogs, and that some combinations simply don't work. It is fine to leave the dog run and come back another time, or take a personal, one-on-one walk with your dog in the neighborhood and come back in a few minutes to see if the run has emptied out a bit.

2.

Consider leaving your cell phone off, or not taking calls, unless it's an emergency, during your dog's time at the dog run. The more attention you give your dog, and the more you participate, the better the relationship. This is a good time for you and your dog to be together, and doesn't your dog deserve your undivided attention?

3.

Make sure your dog's play partner(s) are playing fair, and that your own dog is playing fair, too. This means that each dog takes turns pushing and initiating physical contact (being on top) and that neither dog is pushing another dog relentlessly. There should be frequent role reversals in healthy play.

4.

Make sure your own dog is actually playing with another dog, and not just responding in a defensive, deflective way based on fear. Call your dog to you, and when you release him to go back to "play", see if he indeed does return to engage with the same dog(s). If not, he may not have felt that what he was previously experiencing was really playful or fun for him.

5.

Watch your own dog, and make sure he is not targeting ONE other dog exclusively and going after that particular dog relentlessly—even if you think your dog is "just playing". Playing is a balance between the dogs, a give and take—not one dog pushing and jumping and mouthing the other dog over and over and over again. If your dog is doing this to another dog, go and get him, or call him to you and get him under control. The same holds true if your dog is the target of another dog's obsession. Go and rescue your dog from the situation.

6.

Watch out for "ganging" up: when two or more dogs "gang up" and relentlessly chase or surround another dog. Have all the owners call their dogs, and probably one or more of the gang members should leave the run for that time, as they'll usually start back up again.

7.

Toy dogs should play with other toy or small-ish dogs, and should absolutely not be in the run with the big dogs. A predatory attack can happen instantly and without warning. The risk to toy dogs is too great.

8.

Beware of high-speed games of chase. Alone, two dogs playing chase is probably fine, but if other dogs join in, then a high-speed game of chase can arouse other dogs, and in an instant this can turn into a predatory attack. It's hard to get control once dogs begin this high-speed chase, which is why you want to catch it early, and why you want to spend a lot of time training your dog in the run. You want control when your dog starts to get out of control. But you can't wait until he is out of control to train your dog to listen to you. Train him while he is relatively calm.

9.

Participate in your dog's playtime. Interrupt every few minutes by calling your dog to you, rewarding with at least one treat every two seconds, and keep your dog with you for at least 10 seconds. For this entire 10 seconds, praise, pet and reward your dog often enough so that he doesn't have a chance to look away from you. This encourages attention, and allows your dog to calm down and focus on a human in between aroused playtimes.

10.

Playing with other dogs is very, very fun for your dog, sometimes more fun than being with people, and sometimes more fun than being with YOU. This puts you at a disadvantage in every other situation with your dog. It is important to include yourself in your dog's play activities. Watch your dog, encourage your dog, interrupt your dog, play with your dog.

11.

Call your dog to come to you frequently, not just when it's time to leave. By calling him over to you frequently, rewarding him with something valuable, and then releasing him back to play, you can avoid the difficulty many Dog Park frequenters experience: the dog who can't be caught when it's time to leave. Make sure that calling your dog to come to you doesn't just signal the time to leave. By calling him and having him sit by your side, receive your praise and petting for a brief time before releasing him with permission to go back and play teaches your dog that coming to you is merely a pleasant interruption, and not an end to his fun.

NOTES:

Printed by Amazon Italia Logistica S.r.l.
Torrazza Piemonte (TO), Italy

16936829R00050